Jonathan and Evie's Autumn

Holly Evelyn Rogers

BookLeaf
Publishing

India | USA | UK

Presentation by *BookLeaf Publishing*

Web: www.bookleafpub.com

E-mail: info@bookleafpub.com

ISBN: 9789363301214

First edition 2024

*For My Kindred, My Same-Cloth, My Love- you
are still, and ever, the Ink the gives me voice,
and My Eternal Autumn.*

Love's Grasp (2009/2024)

The Hands of Time did wind
But they could not unbind
 Your Love's grasp on me

Within the forced feigning of our death
In the Turning away from Our Sun
It let out a ragged Breath
Crying
No, Mine, It is not done.
Weeping to fill the chasm
Stretched o'er eight Summers' bleakness
It's gentle hands through Hair and Soul
Suffered not a weakness
It grew in Autumn's Quiet
And cut through Black of Days
It sang through Hot and Night-
 Whispered in broken prayers

My Name upon Its Tongue
My Faith fast in Its Hold
It waited at the Altar
Believing in Autumn's Gold

Till I did reach and break the lock
Sprinting miles to Your Door

My shoes worn through, You lifted me
With Eyes and Arms most sure

Indelible Ink fell from Our Sky
Autumn's Song within Its Rain
Among the Pines Love breathed again
And united us by Name.

Anthropomorphic

Yours is the Face that God wears
When He wants me to believe
He is Love.

Narcissus' Daughters (2024)

How many years of Light till the dark creeps in?
I fought to hold it back
But I was letting it in.

Every place where I am "thin"
And weak.

You are Stars
And Sun
And Moon

And what Light I have is yours.
I was raised at Night
I have memorized the Shadows.
That is how I'm still alive.

But you
Need Day
And Order
And food

You must surely look back from the table
And see my Sword
Poised to kill dead shadows
Rescuing from Darkness that has has fled

But I don't know It's dead.
I think it finds me everywhere

Even Here
Where you are
Where I survive-
Where you Live.

Where I am still trying to save Them
While they drown
In Yesterday's Flood.

I fear their Water is between Us
(From my Rain)
Do You love an Autumnal Desert
That I cannot give?

Do you tire of the drowning swim
That invades Your peace?

Where your resources die
And do not yet Save?

I want to be Your Light-
Your Home
Your Peace

Yet my power fades.
I didn't mean to spread Your Light

Four Persons wide
And break It into shadows.

Yet I love you more than Two Thousand and
Nine
And deeper than Trouble's Waters

I fight to keep you bouyant
While You love Narcissus' Daughters

The Weaving

Dying, that Summer
As many before
Barely breathing
 In the Blackness of Its Brightness
And then a Flicker
Of Gold.
A rush of Breath
In keystrokes,
A connection of Threads on single Loom
Intertwined-
The smoothest Weft and Warp
Became a Fabric
Two Beings
Cut from the Same Cloth-
Joined
Turning Summer into Autumn

Epiphany

The last Morning
I sat on the edge of the hotel bed
The TV murmuring over the sound of Your
shower.
Trying to absorb our final Moments
Instead of drowning in the Terror of his arrival.

You walked past me, in a towel
An utter Absence of chaos
 Serenity coloring your eyes
With the Music of lapping waves and gentle rain
And sleepy sighs-
And I knew.

I knew that I had lived to Be with You.
That You would eternally exhale Peace
And make the mundane Divine.

Native Language

An alien, I was, in my father's house
An Orphan at his table
A withered leaf on his family tree
For his brothers to wipe their boots on

A Prison-Sister to my mother
(I Mothered, though a child)
Illegitimate beneath the World's withering gaze

No Homeland, was there, beyond that Door
(Though slim and self-erasing)
No Friend or Love or Voice of God
Anathema, my Name

And then A Voice
Of Gold and Leaf
In the language of My Fibers

Asked of me,
"Is it You?"
And bid me to a Waking

2009

My Most Sacred Memory
Came back to Me
He gave Me His Name amongst the Trees
At Summer's last breath
And Autumn's First Light
We vowed in Ink
There would be no night
Of separation
No more years of unknowing
We asked of Her,
Autumn, please give us a Slowing
Of Days
Of Touches and Breaths
I, without Him, shall refuse all rest
Tall Pines, make a Portal
Push our Souls through
Stay Us as One
Eternity Through

My Kindred (2018)

When All my Days tremble beneath
Suffocation's weight,
In Your eyes is the Fullest, Deepest Breath
When one thousand touches have aimed to force
my Pleasure, pressing me to cry for the dark
Mercy of Death,
Your New hands leave me pleading for the sun
to hold it's place.
Your sudden presence is known by my Soul and
my skin, before my eyes have even taken You
in-
All of me knows that You are in the place where
I am, and hungers to close the smallest gap.
Daily, the sun ascends by the Fuel of Hope,
Descending in a Peace of unknown colors.
This, simply, because I share Your Name.
You are my Comfort to let go of misplaced
Faith,
My Steel to ask impossible questions,
And my new-born Courage to walk Unclothed.
You are my Homeland, My Kindred.
At any moment, I would stride strongly through
Flames next to you
Than recline in soft riches with any other Being.

The Way To You, Part I

The Grey of Dim crowded in
 To days that were already Night
Squeezing out whole Memory,
Will, and Appetite
Two decades of Skull-Clutching Received a
Name
Throwing me to the ground
The Passive One-
The Flight, not the Fight
(That's Me-)
Donned a cape bestowed by Providence.
Withering and wretching
Falling and Praying
Psalm 91
Again and Again
A flicker of God
"Don't wipe out the Light"
Ten Hours of Precision-Battle
I escaped The Door-
Awoke to Grey-less Day
To small Faces that didn't know
And to Satan,
Who was not finished

The Way to You, Part II

Fog and Pain and Nightless Days
A Flesh-Rope on Smooth Scalp.
The Flash of Victory lost its Light
And died in The House of No Windows

Crumbling of Mountain Top
Pounding Heart, Quickening Breath
Unexpected War
(I Lived to Die by Intimate Hands?)
My Delicate Flowers-
The Small Faces
Were Breaking by the Moment

"I can live to help Them run"
That is Enough.
He pursued
And Trespassed-
One more Scar in my Constellation
(What happened to My Fight?)

And While I gasped for Breath,
In Broke Autumn's Light

The Way to You, Part III

Spirit broke from Body,
There on Summer's floor
She fled, like Urgent Prayer
To rap on Autumn's Door.

Would You answer,
(Would You hear?)
Would Your arms be full?
In want of Resurrection,
She sought her Kindred Soul.

Three Decades of Dreams at Your Threshold
(God, let this One Thing Be-)
The Door swung open
To frame You there,
Alone beneath Our Tree.

Green met Green in Gaze of Fire
Ink quick, began to stir
Spirit safe, joined Body
Enveloped in Gold Blur.

Whole, I drank You In-
From the Cup Which Autumn Gives
This,

Our Season,
You My Love-
You are why I Lived.

Chaste

I never fought for Your Eyes-
For Your Love
Our Soul's kissed before we spoke Our names.
You Saw me
(You looked deep-)
At first sight.
You
I
Heard Your Native Tongue
And that's what turned Your Head.
Not Breasts
Not Legs
Not Edge.
You recognized the Song I sang-
It was written for You.
For Your Ears, Your Hands
Your Mouth.
The Song in My throat-
And nothing else
(Or Less)
Called You into Season.
Heaven's Mystery, it was-
Heaven's Music.
My breasts, My legs, so weary,
So burdened by their Task

Laid down and wept.
And After Sonnets and Songs-
At Day of Symphony the First,
They found the Strength to Reach
And meet Your skin.
How we ever refrained, I'll not know
But the Knowing of Your Restraint
Begat Years of Passion We Now Taste.

You

Sweet, Your lips
And deep their taste
Telling words unspoken
Across my skin
Their Song begins
Every inch awoken

Soft, Your hands
And Soft, They Beckon
Cries of Yes and Now
They ask for nothing
Content to Dance
Unaware, Their Power

Sure, my Answer
(Only for You-)
The Composer of Our Suite
A Moment, Awaited
Now unfolds
In Autumn's Golden Heat

Indelible

The Cutting Away cleared Memory-
Of Book, and Film, and Friend
Yet spared me All of You
So we could Know again.
Remember?
My finger-trace down Your back,
Our Feet in Winter Light
My Hair Spread out across Your Chest
Your beckoned Kiss at Night.
Lemon cake before Rachmaninoff,
Releasing the Bouquet
And Cars, and Bridges,
And Somewhere in Time-
A Lunch Note for each day.
Airports, and vans, and Weeping
The Parting
(We survived)
To recite it All in Married Bed
Together and Alive

Weaver

Early, there was a Breaking
From Flesh to Spirit through-
And broken, I remained
Til You came breathing through.

A Dream I dared not weave,
A Hope that I had killed
A Friendship of Good Stars
No Ancestor could will.

They were Broken, also-
By men of half-weaved cloth
Who tore Them in their Tearing
Giving garments of Sackcloth.

Each did wear such Curse
We could only play this part-
Till your Weaving Hands brought
Healing
To a Lineage of Hearts

Here ends trait of Rending
Of boots upon soft Souls
You turned the Key
For More than Me
And made the Broken Whole.

One

All I knew of was the Taking
(The First Time, and The Next-)
And then, June-Day,
You entered
With unknown, soft Caress.
Your Eyes that promised
There was no Lie
(No Lie in You, Through and Through)
Your Eyes Pure Streams of Washing,
My whole Being bathed in You.

Your hands reached just to Give
Your Kiss, The Only One
Which made my Longing Live
Unclothed in Autumn Sun.

To Barren Land, now surged a Rush
Composing Verse of Flesh
Which Sang in Nights
And Days
And Hours
Two Threads
One single Mesh.

Wanting

I always want You,
And that is Heavy.
It Has never been safe
to be in Longing.

 (Your Wanting
Moves and Wanes
In some effortless flow
No sign of work, that I can see,
It is a Ghost I cannot hold)

My Fear, She writes my Script-
She remembers how It goes
From Times and Men before You
That turned all Longings into Woes.

Never has such Wanting
Coursed the Depths of me
Still I demand It Ask
Before I let You see

I must Decide,
And Relent.
It must Obey
(I cannot help-)

Forever this Dance,
This Game of Roulette
This Deciding to lower The Shield

Acquiesing to be Unclothed
Before knowing how You feel.

Its not an Exchange
Nor a Transaction-
But a Rending and a Sewing
Of Fragile Fabric
Which can bear no stress
I cannot will a Foregoing

I cannot turn my Face from the Definition
Of joining my Body to Yours-
It is All Things-
It is Gospel and it is Glory
Its Elixir, worth these Wars

Seven years,
It has not altered
But ease I'll not pursue-
I'd unpick the Fibers of My Soul
To Wed myself to You

Autumn's Queen

I was more than Robert's Francesca-
More than Richard's Elise
I was New Autumn in Your Summer
I was sole Muse to My Only Ink

What else is there to covet?
What more could I dream?
This is Light from Beyond-
We are Divinity's Theme

Dare it cool into some August,
I possess One irrevocable Gift
I was the Dearest Evie
To My Precious Jonathan Swift

Roots

Like Sunrise
And Tides,
As Clocks
And measured Time,
You are Unwavering.

Never straying from my Eyes,
You walk the Cleanest Line
Gifting calm Night
And Gentle Morning.

This Security of Angels
Wraps Child-Hearts in soft blanket
In Newborn Light
They reach to take it.

They rest in Our Rest
(Their first Shielded Nest)
And from Our lungs They are full-breathing.

They have no want
In Soul or Hand,
They fear no House-Storm, now
This Home You have made
Quiet and Stayed

Deftly hidden in Autumn's Bough

It's given New Day-
It has dared Them to Play
As reborn, and free from Bother

Do You see All of this?
Your bestowed, Quiet Gift-
You,
 Their Truest
Their Surest Father.

Dayenu

A dance of Sonnets and Verse
Of Prose and Conversation;
 And yet, I needed Your voice.

Pavlov and sighing and whispers
Stolen Minutes of Voice in ear;
But I longed to see Your Face.

Images exchanged, passed across miles
Moving pictures of Face and Voice;
Still I ached to touch my lips to Your temple.

Measured caresses and Eyes and Hair
Skin pressing Skin, against Limit
We wept to become One.

A Wedding among the Pines
Minutes, and Seasons, and Years
It's All The Things,
And yet not Enough
God, let Us own Forever.

Autumn's Vow 2017

A flurry of keystrokes-
A flash of a Moment,
Our Souls recognized their Native Language.
"Kindred", the pressured whisper reached both
of Our ears.
There, within Your words, I recognized my
Homeland
There, within Your Autumn,
My Endless Summer died away.
Bare branches of Souls, intertwined
Inextricably.
I Vow to You, Love
To never forget-
To shower You with Remembering.
Indelible, that first Sound of Your Voice
Splitting the Glass Room of Silence.
Your Light rushed in,
And I Breathed.
I will Forever find You, at any cost-
Look at You with Kindred Eyes,
Even if searching in the Dark.
The Dream of Us will renew at Each Waking,
and find me building, and reaching and holding.
I refuse to find Us Common or Faded.
Never will I stop Winning You,

And the Prize of Your Soul Entangled in Mine.
I will Stay-
All of Me,
All The Days.
I Marry You today to be Married to All that You
Are,
To Endlessly be Same-Cloth, spread across the
Table of Our Days.
In Me, forever, You will find Your Advocate,
And a heart that swells to look upon Your Face.
Our hands, Eternally holding, our Eyes, Ever
Assuring.
I ask, Forever, to Be Your Caretaker,
Your Kindred,
And Your Muse.
You have Ever been, and tirelessly remain
My Ink, My Kindred,
My Lone Habitant in Summer's Glass Room.
From Autumn's Dawn until The Door,
You Alone are My Home-
The Only Place where I am Known.